# Will I Make It To Heaven...

**Jason O'Neal Williams**
**"Prince Jason"**
**The Prince of Poetry**

**Will I Make It To Heaven?**

A Royalistic Ink Book

Published by arrangement with the author Jason O'Neal Williams and in association with Royalistic Ink.

Copyright © 2008 by Royalistic Ink. Cover design by Royalistic Ink and Brandon Jenkins. This book, or parts thereof, may not be reproduced in any form without permission. All rights reserved.

**Brandon Jenkins**

> **Experience**

Illustrating, pencils, inking and painting

> **Email address**

bitterartist@gmail.com

**Editor**

Jason O'Neal Williams
"Prince Jason"
The Prince of Poetry and Storytelling

2002 International Poet of the Year nominee
2002 International Poet Merit Award
2002 Editor's Choice Award
1st Published book, **My Story, "Through My Eyes"** (2003) Publish America
2nd Published book, **E.3** (**E**xperiencing Death, **E**motional Disturbance, **E**verlasting Love) 2004- Publish America
2003 Appearance in Ebony magazine
2004 Pinkie Carolyn Wilkerson Award for Literacy and Poetry- Presented to him by Grambling State University
2004 International Who's Who In Poetry-The only American featured poet for that year
3rd Published book, **The Life That I Live** (2005) Publish America
4th Published book, **I Must Confess, "The Lost Pages"** (2005) Publish America
5th Published book, **2 Sides To A Story** (2005) Publish America

2006 Pinkie Carolyn Wilkerson Award for Literacy and Poetry- Presented to him by Grambling State University

6th Published book, **Prince Jason, "Welcome to my Kingdom"** (2007) Starving Writers Publishing

7th book, **7** (2008) Starving Writers Publishing/Royalistic Ink

8th book, **J.B.3.** (2008) Royalistic Ink

9th book, **J.B.3 Coloring Book** (2008) Royalistic Ink

10th book, **Will I Make It To Heaven?** (2008) Royalistic Ink

## Websites

www.myspace.com/prince_jason
www.authorsden.com/princejason
www.authorsden.com/jb3

## Email address

majortalent2003@yahoo.com
onealwill@yahoo.com

**Expression**

First given honor to God. I can do all things through Jesus who strengthens me. This poetry book is a collection of spiritual poems that I've written for the past 5 years. These poems are published in my previous books. I know I'm not perfect, I do and done wrong stuff. But I know that God is forgiveness. If you stop your evil ways, you are forgiving. God will forgive you. I know now that I have to be a better Christian. Each day I live, I will get better and show others what God wants them to see. Open up your hearts and let God in. It will change and save your life.

*Prince Jason*

## About The Author

Jason O'Neal Williams, also known as Prince Jason "The Prince of Poetry and Storytelling" was born July 21, 1978 in Houston Texas. His education is in Marketing and Literature to which he studied at Grambling State University, he graduates in 2002. He is a Poet, Author, Professional Writer Speaker, Editor, Producer, Columnist, Literary Agent, Screenwriter, Actor and CEO of Royalistic Ink.

He has appeared in Ebony Magazine in 2003 and was a poetry writer for Black College Today Magazine. Jason has been awarded the 2004 Pinkie Carolyn Wilkerson Award - Literacy and Poetry, Grambling State, 2006 Pinkie Carolyn Wilkerson Award - Literacy and Poetry, Grambling State 2004 International Who's Who In Poetry nominee-The only American featured poet for that year, 2002 International Poet of the year nominee, 2002 International Poet of Merit award, January 2002 Editor's choice award.

He has published poem "I Want To Succeed" in poetry anthology,

"Solitude" (2002), Published poem "Rain" in poetry anthology, "New Millennium Poets" (2002), Published poem "We Are Poets" in poetry anthology, "International Who's Who In Poetry" (2004).

Jason's Books are:

- ✓ 1st Book: "My Story, Through My Eyes" (2003) Publish America
- ✓ 2nd Book: "E.3" (Experiencing Death, Emotional Disturbance, Everlasting Love) 2004- Publish America
- ✓ 3rd book The Life That I Live (2005) Publish America
- ✓ 4th book I Must Confess, "The Lost Pages" (2005) Publish America
- ✓ 5th book, 2 Sides To A Story (2005) Publish America
- ✓ 6th book Prince Jason, Welcome to my Kingdom (2007) Starving Writers Publishing
- ✓ 7th book 7 (2008) Starving Writers Publishing/Royalistic Ink
- ✓ 8th J.B.3 (2008) Royalistic Ink
- ✓ 9th book, J.B.3 Coloring Book (2008) Royalistic Ink

- ✓ 10th book, Will I Make It To Heaven? (2008) Royalistic Ink

**Table of Contents**

**My Religion**                  12

| | |
|---|---|
| Rain | 13 |
| A Kiss to the Sky | 14 |
| Calling on You | 16 |
| G-O-D | 19 |
| Help Me Lord | 20 |
| My Guardian Angel | 21 |
| God Is With Me | 23 |
| I Need God | 25 |
| I Need You Father | 27 |
| Show Me The Light | 29 |
| Satan Is Tempting Me | 31 |
| The Life of a Sinner | 33 |
| Follow God's Light | 37 |

**My Conversation With God**    40

| | |
|---|---|
| My Spirit | 41 |
| We Lost Our Way | 42 |
| God's Light | 44 |
| God's Sacrifice | 45 |
| I Believe In God | 47 |
| God Is Watching | 48 |
| God Is Love | 49 |
| Resisting The Devil | 51 |
| I Love The Lord | 53 |
| Let Not Your Heart Be Troubled | 55 |
| Confessing My Sins | 57 |
| I'm Free | 59 |
| My Conversation With God | 60 |

**Just Begun**                    63

| | |
|---|---|
| Surviving Death | 64 |
| The Way I Act | 65 |
| I'm Losing My Religion | 67 |
| Just Begun | 69 |
| I'm Not Ready For It | 70 |
| Keep Me Together | 71 |
| Why Are You Testing Me? | 73 |
| I Can't Let This Go | 75 |
| Will Never Move Along | 77 |

## Thinking About Church    78

| | |
|---|---|
| My God | 79 |
| I Believe In God | 81 |
| Thank You | 83 |
| I'm Down On My Knees | 85 |
| To God | 87 |
| My Letter To God | 88 |
| Show Me Lord | 90 |
| This I Pray | 92 |
| Follow | 94 |
| I Hear You God | 96 |
| I Know God | 99 |
| The Mark That You Left | 100 |
| Thinking About Church | 101 |

## I'm Praying For My Life Back    103

| | |
|---|---|
| I'm Praying For My Life Back | 104 |
| I Told God I'll Be Back | 110 |
| Run With Patience | 112 |
| Reading The Bible | 114 |
| I'm Incomplete | 117 |
| Speak Up And Talk | 119 |
| The Devil Goes To Church | 121 |
| Spiritual High | 123 |

Putting My Life Back Together   126
Heaven                         129
Is There a Place For Me In Heaven?
       131
**My Story**                   **133**
**Author's Accomplishments**   **141**

# My Religion

My religion is a part of me
God is showing me the way to
be
My faith
My belief
My religion is my key to relief

## **Rain**

Rain
God's tears of love
Rain
God's tears from above

Rain
Tears from above
Rain washed away my hate
God purified me with his love

Rain washed away my pain
Now I have glee
Rain washed away all my misery

Rain washed away my despair and sadness
Rained washed away my insanity and madness

Rain
A peaceful sight
Rain
Tears of right

Rain
God's tears of love
Rain
God's tears from above

## **A Kiss to the Sky**

I do this anytime
I do this on any occasion
I blow a kiss to the sky
To show God my appreciation

Everyday I blow a kiss to the sky
Thanking God for not letting life
pass me by

I do this
To show respect
I do this
So I won't forget
That I'm here
I'm living
Thanking him for
What he's giving

The ability
That I have inside me
The ability to be all
That I can be

I do this
Out of love
I do this to thank him
For the miracles that are sent from
above

I do this to honor those
Who passed away
I do this to honor those
Who are not here today

I do this anytime
I do this on any occasion
I blow a kiss to the sky
To show God my appreciation

**Calling on You**

"We"
Which means together
Lord
I will praise you forever

I'm calling for guidance
I'm calling for assistance
Lord
I'm calling with no resistance

Lord
I call on you to help me
Lord
I call on you to help me see
Which way to go
Because I'm confused right now
I really don't know

The devil is on my back
The devil is leading me off track
Satan is showing me no kind of slack

The devil fills me with
Anger and despair
The devil don't love me
Satan don't care

But I know that your love is
everlasting
Forever
Your love brings out the best in me
Your love keeps me together

I should call on you Lord
When I'm not in need
I should call on you for any reason
This indeed

Lord, we've been through a lot
I thank you for not forsaking me
when I question your actions
And when my soul was raging hot

Lord, you know that we go through
our stages
Kind to mean
Our emotional rages

Emotional rage means
Acting out your pain
Expressing these emotions
Because it's hard to contain

Emotional rage
The bad feelings that we keep inside
Lord thank you for saving my life
Because I almost died

Lord without you
My soul is lost
Lord I know that your love has no cost

"We"
Which means together
Lord
I will praise you forever

### G-O-D

My Lord
**G-O-D**
Is the one
We all need to see

**G-Goodness**
**O-Overcomes**
**D- Darkness**
Do you know what I mean?
Be good
And your soul will stay clean

God is my way
When I'm lost
I don't have to pay for his love
It's free with no cost

Evil
You must let go
Resist Satan
Just say no

My Lord
**G-O-D**
Is the one
We all need to see

## Help Me Lord

Get away from me Satan
I'm not going your way
Lord, give me strength
This I pray

Forgive me Lord
I making a plea
Guide me Lord
So I can see
That evil is not the way to go
Show me Lord
Let me know

Teach me Lord
Help me understand
Reach out to me Lord
Give me your hand

My Lord, My Savior
Show me what's right
Give me strength
Help me fight

Get away from me Satan
I'm not going your way
Lord, give me strength
This I pray

## My Guardian Angel

I know angels exist
I know they do
I believe this
I know it's true

I feel you
Whenever you're near
You're by my side
I'm glad you're here

You were there
At my birth
You're here with me now
On this earth

You give me strength
You give me confidence
You are my perception
Another sense

You're with me
Every step I take
You prevent me from making a
crucial mistake

You always whisper some advice in
my ear
You always tell me
There's nothing to fear

You will never leave my side
You are my direction
You are my guide

You will always stand up
And have my back
We will face anything together
You will never lead me off track

We can face any situation together
My guardian angel is my protector forever

My guardian angel
Will never let me fall
My guardian angel
Is always on the call

With you by my side
I know that everything will be all right
You are my eyes
When I lose sight

I know angels exist
I know they do
I believe this
I know it's true

## God Is With Me

I know this with certainty
God is definitely with me

When it's dark
And I lose sight
God becomes my eyes
He is my light

When Satan tempts me to do wrong
Instead of right
God is my will
He gives me the strength to fight

When this cold world turns on me
And push me away
God will take me in
His house will be my place to stay

My heart no longer suffers or strain
Because I've found peace through
God
That relieved all my pain

I no longer worry or fear
Because God will always be near

I no longer question or dwell
Because heaven is my place
And not hell

I know this with certainty
God is definitely with me

# I Need God

You're my everything
You're my all
You're the one
I can always call

God help me
Help me see
I need your help to become the person
I need to be

Guide me
Show me the way
Hold my hand
So I can't get away

Hold me
Don't let go
When I'm doing wrong
Let me know

God help me
I need some saving
It's your love
That I'm craving

God
Don't let me fall
Help me
My back is against the wall

You're my everything
You're my all
You're the one
I can always call

## **I Need You Father**

I can always call on you
I know it's not a bother
I need you God
I need you father

I need you father
Everyday
I need you father
That's why I pray

I need you father
To let me in
I need you father
To help me fight sin

I need you father
Because I'm weak
I need you father
It's help that I seek

I need you father
This road is becoming too hard to bear
I need you father
To show me love and care

I need you father
To forgive me
I need you father
Because I'm blind and can't see

I've lost sight of what's right
I've lost the strength to fight
I need you father
Day and night

I can always call on you
I know it's not a bother
I need you God
I need you father

## Show Me The Light

I'm confused
I need some insight
Show me the way
Show me the light

What is my direction?
Where do I need to go?
What must I learn?
What must I know?

Which way should I travel?
Which way should I explore?
What road should I take?
Where is the door?
That I need to go through
Please help me
I need a clue

What must I do?
What must I give?
To help me understand
New ways to live

I'm confused
I need some insight
Show me the way
Show me the light

## **Satan Is Tempting Me**

Hell
Is not the place to be
Hell
Is not the place for me

Satan
Get off my back
Get away from me
Stop trying to throw me off track

Satan
You're not going to turn off my light
I'm going to fight you
With all my might

Stop trying to tempt me
Stop trying to persuade me
Leave me alone
Let me be

This time
You won't lead me away
This time
I won't stray

Satan
Why do you exist?
I can't give in
I must resist

I'm ready
Let's go
God's on my side now
You better know
That you can't win
The Lord is leading me
Away from sin

Satan is persistent
Satan won't quit
Satan wants my soul
My soul
Satan is trying to get

Satan
I'm not listening to you anymore
My destiny is heaven
I will be at that door
To receive God
You can't stop me from being with
God

Hell
Is not the place to be
Hell
Is not the place for me

## The Life of a Sinner

You will go through this
Sin will challenge you
The life of a sinner
A poem about the sins that we do

I'm a sinner
I will sin
I will do anything
And everything to win

I commit crimes
I steal
Goodness
Is something that I don't feel

I'm bad
I'm evil
I'm wild
I'm not civil

I love greed
I will take from you
Because that's my nature
Something that I do

I don't care about nothing
I don't care about you
My attitude is contagious
Like the flu

Sin flows through my body
Everyday
Evil flows through my body
In everyway

It's hard to figure out
Why sin exist
When sin tempts you
It's hard to resist

Sinners
Are never winners
Sinners are veterans
And beginners

Sin is all over the place
Sin is something
That you will face
While you're here
Sin will linger
And stay near

Murder
Lying
Stealing
Trying
To break a law so odd
Like breaking the laws of God

A sinner don't listen
A sinner don't care
We all sin
Sinners are everywhere

Sinners are destructive
Violent
Sinners are loud
Sinners are silent

I am a sinner
The devil is in me
The devil is showing me
New ways to be

Evil
Mad
Angry
Bad

Sin is showing me
A new light
Sin is showing me
The opposite of right

Sin
The other part
Sin
Darkens the heart

I love sin
I hope sin never goes away
I hope sin last
I hope sin is here to stay

You will go through this
Sin will challenge you
The life of a sinner
A poem about the sins that we do

## Follow God's Light

I'm resisting the devil
With all of my might
I will always do what's right and never lose sight
I will follow God's light

When my heart was in pain
God was there
When this cold world pushed me down
God picked me up because he care

It's not fair
Out there
Don't let the devil blind you
Watch out for the devil's glare

God is my direction
God is my way
I will trust in the Lord
Everyday

I will not listen to the devil
Satan will not tempt me
Leave me alone devil
Let me be

That day
When I was down and out
God erased all the bad thoughts
inside my mind
God eliminated all the doubt
About life
God healed my heart
God removed all the strife

God loves me
God truly do
God will always see me through

I called out to God
God heard my cry
God helped me
God didn't pass me by

God
Wiped away all my tears
God
Removed all my fears

I have courage now
I can do all things
I'm ready for whatever life brings

I pray every night
To the Lord up above
To send down all his love
Because we need it everyday
Lord, please take my pain away

This world is filled with so much sin
The devil is trying to win

The devil is trying to conquer
And take control
The devil is trying to take my soul

I'm resisting the devil
With all of my might
I will always do what's right and
never lose sight
I will follow God's light

# My Conversation With God

Speak to me God
I pray everyday
My conversation with God
What I have to say

## My Spirit

God keeps me strong
God helps me strive
My heart is filled with so much joy
My spirit is alive

When I'm with God
I'm happy and filled with glee
Because I know
God loves me

My spirit has rejoiced in God
My Savior
God is merciful
God forgives my behavior

God keeps me strong
God helps me strive
My heart is filled with so much joy
My spirit is alive

## **We Lost Our Way**

I'm telling you what I know
Hear what I say
We're going in the opposite direction
We lost our way

In today's society
The devil is very much in charge
The devil is unleashed
The devil is at large

Senseless dying
Killing each other
Love
Is not shown enough to one another

Everyday violence
The distribution of drugs
Every arguments and fights
There's no more smiles and hugs

Wars
Sin
We're walking on frail ice
The ice is thin

Breaking God's commandments
Church attendance decrease
So much hate
Not enough peace
We know it's not right
But we won't stop or cease

I'm telling you what I know
Hear what I say
We're going in the opposite direction
We lost our way

## **God's Light**

The light gives me insight
On ways to fight
The light is my direction
When it's dark as night

I see it
I'm seeing the light
I'm starting to see what's right

I see it
It's showing me the way
It leads me
So I won't stray

The light
Shines in my face
The light
Takes me away from this place

The light gives me insight
On ways to fight
The light is my direction
When it's dark as night

## God's Sacrifice

God sacrificed his only son
Because he loves us so much
I'm filled with the Holy Spirit
I feel God's touch

God sacrificed his only son to save
us
From sin
We can't allow the devil to take over
We can't allow the devil to win

Did we forget about this?
Don't you care?
We have to wake up
Because the devil is everywhere

God sacrificed his own son because
he loves us
He wants us to love each other
He wants us to take care of each
other
God wants us to have compassion
for one another

God sacrificed his only son
To save our soul
God sacrificed his only son
So the devil won't take control

God sacrificed his only son
So we could have everlasting life
I believe in God, My Savior
Because with the devil, there's always strife

God sacrificed his only son
Because he loves us so much
I'm filled with the Holy Spirit
I feel God's touch

## I Believe In God

I will follow his direction
God is showing me what's right
I believe in God
I will follow his light

I believe in God
God is always near
God gives me courage
So I can face fear

I believe in God
God always have been by my side
I'm going to display my love for him
I will not hide

I will follow his direction
God is showing me what's right
I believe in God
I will follow his light

## **God Is Watching**

We need to stop it right now
While the sky is still clear blue
God doesn't like
The things that we do

God is giving us a chance
To change our ways
But time is almost up
God is counting down the days

Time is almost up
Are you aware?
Time is slipping away
Be aware

I'm not perfect
Not at all
The devil's temptation is all around me
From large to small

We need to stop it right now
While the sky is still clear blue
God doesn't like
The things that we do

**God Is Love**

The fact that he still loves me after
all I've done
Is unconceivable
God is love
God's love is so unbelievable

God is love
This I know
I feel his affection inside of me
I feel his love flow

God is love
God sacrificed his only son for me
With God I am happy
God fills me glee

God is love
The devil is not
Hell is not the place for me
Hell is hot

God is love
I feel is love everyday
God's love is everlasting
His love will always stay

The devil's concern for me is fake
It's not real
The devil don't care about me
I will not take his deal

The fact that he still loves me after
all I've done
Is unconceivable
God is love
God's love is so unbelievable

## Resisting The Devil

My God washes
And cleans all the hate
I'm ready to see the devil lose
I just can't wait

When the devil grabs my leg
I'm just going to kick him off me
When the devil puts his hands over
my eyes
I'm going to move them so I can see

When the devil start whispering in
my ear
I'm just going to shoo him away
I'm not going to believe anything
That the devil say

The devil will not tempt me
I will do no wrong
God is my strength
Through God I'm strong

The devil's temptation is so
appealing
The devil temptation is an
overwhelming feeling

The devil is tricky
The devil will do anything to get you
The devil will try his best to deceive
you

I must resist the devil
I don't want to go his way
I stay down on my knees
Everyday I pray

I'm resisting the devil
There's an on going fight
A battle against
Wrong and right

God protects me
God is my shield
I am aware of the devil's temptation
The sign is yield

This means slow down
Prepare to stop
My God will crush Satan under his
feet
My God cleans my soul with his
mop

My God washes
And cleans all the hate
I'm ready to see the devil lose
I just can't wait

## I Love The Lord

God didn't forsake me
God didn't pass me by
I love the Lord
God heard my cry

God loves me
And I love him
God said, "Love thy enemies"
God said, "Love all of them"

The Lord said, "Love your neighbor"
Even if you don't want to
You have to love and forgive your enemies
This is what you do

I will seek God
Because I need his guidance or direction
God's love
Is the right affection

I put my trust in the Lord
Day after day
My love for God
Will never go away

God didn't forsake me
God didn't pass me by
I love the Lord
God heard my cry

## Let Not Your Heart Be Troubled

I have a problem
Now it's doubled
The Lord told me not to worry
Let not your heart be troubled

Let not your heart be troubled
Because I am here
Don't be afraid
Have no fear

Let not your heart be troubled
Let go of the strife
I sacrificed my only son
So you can have everlasting life

Let not your heart be troubled
Let go of the dread
Hold on and stay strong
Follow the words that I said

Let not your heart be troubled
I know it's bad right now
But you will make it
Some way, some how

Let not your heart be troubled
Pain is not forever
The love that I have for you
Will keep you together

I have a problem
Now it's doubled
The Lord told me not to worry
Let not your heart be troubled

## Confessing My Sins

I'm not a good person
I'm not good at all
I'm surprised
That you heard my call

I am a sinner
I did something bad
I'm a mean person
I make others feel sad

I'm filled with anger
I hate you
I don't care about
What I put you through

I cheat
I steal
I hurt people
I kill

I don't go to church
I don't believe in God
Doesn't that sound strange to you?
Doesn't that sound odd?

I don't attend church like I should
My attendance is low
God will never turn me away
His answer will never be no

I'm a sinner God
Please forgive me
Show me your mercy
Let me see

I'm not a good person
I'm not good at all
I'm surprised
That you heard my call

## I'm Free

Jesus opened my eyes
Now I see
I know
Who I need to be

Jesus
Has set me free
From all of the devil's misery

I'm free
From the laws of sin and death
Jesus has taken me away from the devil
There's been a theft

The spirit of life
Jesus' law
Defrosted my cold heart and soul
Or thaw

Jesus opened my eyes
Now I see
I know
Who I need to be

## **My Conversation With God**

Speak to me God
I pray everyday
My conversation with God
What I have to say

God
How can I get rid of this pain in my life?
God
How can I get rid of this pain that is my life?

God said
"In your darkest hour"
"You will feel my love
"You will feel my power"

God said
"Have faith in me"
"I will show you the way"
"I will help you see"

Killers, murderers
Everyday I'm looking over my shoulder
So much violence
Hate is getting bolder

Fighting against one another
War after war
God
There's really nothing to live for

My body is ill
I have a lasting sickness inside of me
My asthma harasses me everyday
Will I ever be free?

So much death
Constant dying
Too much sadness
Everyone is crying

Deception
So much lying
Can I give up now?
Can I stop trying?

The world is not right
There's so much wrong
Why should I believe in you?
My faith moved along

I'm so upset
I'm so mad
Someone that I know and loved just died
I'm so sad

You took them
You took them from me
There's a huge void in my heart
So much misery

Are you listening God?
Do you hear me?
Are my words clear to thee?

You say everything happens for a reason
Why is this so?
Why does bad stuff always happen?
Please let me know

When I turn on the television
There's no good news
A heart is always breaking
Somebody has the blues

Speak to me God
I pray everyday
My conversation with God
What I have to say

# Just Begun

Talk to me, God
What needs to be done?
The Lord said, have faith
"Your journey just begun"

## Surviving Death

This was a sign
A wake-up call
I saw my life passing me by
I saw it all

My chest hurts
Am I having an asthma attack?
I fainted
I fell on my back

I can't breathe
Where is my air?
I'm not ready to die yet?
This is not fair

Lord, let me live so I can give
And share my poetry
Spare my life
Have mercy on me

This was a sign
A wake-up call
I saw my life passing me by
I saw it all

## The Way I Act

I don't think
Before I react
Back in the day
The way I act

I didn't attend Sunday school
I didn't want to go
Are you going, Jason?
My reply was no

I'm going to morning service
I'm not going to Sunday school
What's wrong with you, Jason?
Stop acting like a fool

I'm not going
So don't ask me anymore
You can't make me
I locked the car door

I'm staying in the car
Until the morning service begin
"God don't like what you're doing"
I'm not committing a sin
This isn't wrong
Now leave me alone
Move along

I don't think
Before I react
Back in the day
The way I act

## I'm Losing My Religion

My downfall
I'm heading for a collision
I made a bad decision
I'm losing my religion

I'm losing my religion
And I don't care
I'm playing by my own rules
Because life is not fair

I'm losing my religion
My faith in God is going away
God is not paying me any attention
God don't watch me each day

What or who is God?
There is no great spiritual power
God doesn't control my fate
God doesn't have any power

Each and every hour
I pray to thee
No answer
God doesn't respond to me

Don't you see?
Don't you know?
Do I still believe in God?
No

Something happened
I'm beginning to change
Something happened
I feel strange

Why did this happen?
Why did this happen to me?
This is meant to be
God wants me to see

I lost my religion
Many times in my life
Now I know that my religion
Is an important part of my life

God didn't forsake me
God didn't let me fall
I can't live without God
I can't do this at all

My faith in God is not small
It's very large
God is the head of my life
God is in charge

My downfall
I'm heading for a collision
I made a bad decision
I'm losing my religion

## Just Begun

Talk to me, God
What needs to be done?
Have faith
Your journey has just begun

Don't tempt me, Satan
That's wrong
So much temptation
It's hard to be strong

Life is hard
Constant punishment
I need some help, God
An angel was sent

Talk to me, God
What needs to be done?
Have faith
Your journey has just begun

### I'm Not Ready

I'm getting upset
I'm starting to have a fit
Something is about to happen
I'm not ready for it

Visions
Dream after dream
All kinds of images
Dream after dream

Why?
What's coming for me?
Why?
What does God want me to see?

I don't know
Show me, God
This is strange to me
This is odd

I'm scared
I'm afraid to sleep
Sleepless nights
I can't sleep

I'm getting upset
I'm starting to have a fit
Something is about to happen
I'm not ready for it

## **Keep Me Together**

The dreams won't stop
It will be like this forever
God is trying
To keep me together

I saw that happen
It came true
God showed me this
God gave me that clue

It bothered me
I was upset
The dream is still here
I can't forget

Dreams
Messages sent to me
From the Lord up above
To help me see

God wants me to know
God wants me to understand
I pray and pray
God, I need your hand

I don't doubt it
I know, I know
God's love is real
It's more than show

The dreams won't stop
It will be like this forever
God is trying
To keep me together

## Why Are You Testing Me?

God, show me the way
Let me see
Let me know
Why the devil is testing me?

Why are you testing me?
With your evil ways
Why do you tempt me with temptation?
I'm not going to embrace your evil ways

For the rest of my days
You will try to persuade me
The devil
Will never let me be

Why are you testing me?
Why are you harassing me?
Lately misery
Is all that I see

Why are you testing me?
Why do you entice?
I can't give in
But it looks so nice

My soul is dirty
It needs to be clean
I can't let my anger take control
I can't be mean

Serene
I need some peace
Eliminate the disturbance inside of me
Let this cease

Satan, the devil
Whoever you are
My door is closed and locked
I won't let you open it or ajar

God, show me the way
Let me see
Let me know
Why the devil is testing me?

## I Can't Let This Go

God is the answer
The Bible tells me so
I can't lose my faith
I can't let this go

I must keep my faith
I have to believe
God won't forsake me
God won't leave

Faith
I lose this time after time
Especially
When I'm down to my last dime

Have faith?
Why?
How will this help?
Why try?

My faith is tested
Each day
Tremendous pain in my knees
Because I continue to pray

Trials
So many trials
My feet are worn out
I've traveled so many miles

It's been so long
What's wrong?
It's hard to survive
It's hard to stay strong

God is the answer
The Bible tells me so
I can't lose my faith
I can't let this go

## Will Never Move Along

I will always maintain
I will stay strong
My faith
Will never move along

The Bible is my weapon
When I fight
God's words
Gave me sight

God's words
Gave me hope to believe
Cured my raging soul
Or relieve

No more pain
No more pain
I've found relief for my heart
God's word took away the pain

I will always maintain
I will stay strong
My faith
Will never move along

# Thinking About Church

Now I realize
Now I know
Church
The place where I can always go

## My God

Do you know God?
I surely do
Lord
I definitely need you

God is my strength
God is my will
God is my cure
For when I'm sick or ill

When I fall
God gives me a hand
When I can't get up
God helps me to stand

God
Your miracles come grand and small
God
I put you above them all

God
You are my demand
When I'm confused
You help me understand

I'm not perfect
I may not do things the right way
But I need you God
Each and every day

Do you know God?
Because I do
Lord
I definitely need you

## **I Believe In God**

Do you understand me?
I don't want to sound odd
I'm full of belief
I believe in God

I believe in God
I have faith in you
Your love and guidance
Will see me through

The devil said that you didn't love me
He lied
The devil tried to trick me
The devil tried
But didn't succeed
It is you God
That I need

You will lead me in the right direction
You will never lead me astray
Your love is forever
Your love for me will never go away

I believe in you God
My faith in you is strong
Show me the right way
Prevent me from doing wrong

Do you understand me?
I don't want to sound odd
I'm full of belief
I believe in God

## Thank You

I'm sincere
I'm telling you something true
I'm very gracious
Lord thank you

I thank you for
Keeping my family near
I thank you for strength and courage
So I can face fear

I thank you for
Allowing me to live
I thank you for
Life that you give

I thank you for
Hope and love
I thank you for
The miracles sent from above

I thank you for
Keeping me fed
I thank you for
Getting me out of bed

I thank you for
Showing me what's right
I thank you for
Showing me the light

I thank you for
Everyday stuff
I thank you for being with me
When life was rough

I thank you for
All the blessings you giving me
I thank you for sight
So I can see

I thank you Lord
I will continue to pray
I thank you Lord
For letting me see another day

I'm sincere
I'm telling you something true
I'm very gracious
Lord thank you

## I'm Down On My Knees

Lord be with me
Lord please stay
I'm down on my knees
I'm kneeling to pray

I'm down on my knees
Because I need to pray
Lord
Please help me today

I'm feeling weak
I'm feeling temptation
I need to resist the devil
I need some preparation

I need to prepare
Because the devil fights dirty
The devil is persuasive
The devil is flirty

The devil will not get me
I won't let the devil win
I will not be fooled
By the devil's inviting grin

The devil will not tempt me
This I won't allow
Because you are my direction Lord
You are showing me how
To resist
I'm happy you're here Lord
I'm glad that you exist

You gave me life
You are my reason for living
You are a caring God
You are also forgiving

Sometimes I get confused
Sometimes I just don't understand
your ways
But I do know your love
Will last the rest of my days

Lord be with me
Lord please stay
I'm down on my knees
I'm kneeling to pray

**To God**

You know who I am
You know the real me
Heaven is where I want to be
You are the one I want to see

Catch me
I'm falling
Answer me
I'm calling

Help me understand
Show me the way
I need you in my life
Everyday

Stop me Lord
Prevent me from sinning
I want the devil to lose
I don't want the devil winning

Show me love
Touch my heart
Don't leave me
I don't want us to be apart

You know who I am
You know the real me
Heaven is where I want to be
You are the one I want to see

## My Letter to God

I believe
I can do all things through you
I believe in God
This is true

Lord
Please hold my hand
As I wonder
Through this mysterious land

This land filled with
Hate and love
I need a miracle
Send one from above

Lord
I know you see it all
You've witness the rise of a person
Or downfall

Lord
I know you are looking down at us
You see the evil things
You see the fuss

You see the arguing, fighting
The killing, lying
The wars
There's too much dying

The drugs that are
Throughout this land
This world is out of control
We are getting out of hand

The sinning
That we all do
I don't see how we made it this far
Do you?

I put my life in your hands Lord
Because I know you will not forsake me
I will not turn my back on you Lord
Because that is not the way to be

Lord
You gave me life
You created love and happiness
And not hate and strife

I believe
I can do all things through you
I believe in God
This is true

## Show Me Lord

Tell me Lord
I need to hear your voice
Show me Lord
The right choice

Lord
Guide me through the night
I need some sight
I need your flashlight

It's dark
I've lost my direction
Lord
I need your affection

Show me love Lord
Show me kindness
Forgive me Lord
For my blindness

The devil is persuading me
The devil is blocking my view
The devil is telling me
I don't need you

But I do
I do need you
Show me the right way
Lord, see me through

I need you Lord
Give me some guidance
Speak to me Lord
Don't leave me with silence

Tell me Lord
I need to hear your voice
Show me Lord
The right choice

**This I Pray**

Speak to me Lord
Day after day
Hear my cry
This I pray

I need you Lord
I need you so much
Cure my pain
With your healing touch

I'm filled with stress
Unbelievable strain
I've lost the desire to live
I forgot how to maintain

My heart is broken
Because it feels no love
Will I fail and go to hell?
Or join you up above?

I need to resist sin
But it's so hard to do
I need to resist the devil
So I can join you

People treat me wrong
They treat me bad
They make me sad
They make me mad

But I can't give in to hate
I have to love my enemy
Because unconditional love
Is God's remedy

I feel reborn
This feels like a fresh start
Because I introduced God into my life
And my heart

I need you God
Because you are the way
Show me the direction to heaven
I need you Lord everyday

Speak to me Lord
Day after day
Hear my cry
This I pray

**Follow**

I'm empty inside
I'm very hollow
God spoke to me
The Lord told me to follow

I'm going through hell
Life is bringing me down
I'm always mad
I have a permanent frown

If you push my buttons
You will release my anger
The caution light will come on
The signal displays danger

The Lord said, "Follow me"
"I will take you there"
"Follow my heart"
"It will lead you to care"

Lord
Give me the strength to fight
Give me the knowledge
To determine what's right

At times I lose sight
And act in a foolish way
But you bring me back
With the words that you say

The Lord said, "Follow me"
"Follow my lead"
"I'll be your gardener"
"I'll pull out every weed"

The Lord said, "Follow me"
"Walk toward the light"
"I'll give you some air"
"When your lungs become tight"

The Lord said, "Follow me"
"I will not lead you wrong"
"Have faith"
"The connection we have is strong"

I'm empty inside
I'm very hollow
God spoke to me
The Lord told me to follow

## **I Hear You God**

I'm not ignoring the advice
That you whisper in my ear
I hear you God
I hear you loud and clear

Come home
Come to my place
This area has unlimited love
And amazing grace

God is in me
I feel the Holy Spirit
I'm not afraid of God's power
anymore
I don't fear it

Do you hear it?
Do you hear God calling?
Are you going to stand up for God?
Or just keep falling?

I'm tired
I'm not going to church today
I see you next week
Next Sunday

I'm not going to church tomorrow
I'm going to the nightclub tonight
Does this sound familiar?
Does this sound right?

Church is boring
Church is not fun
This is only the beginning
The devil just begun

I'm not going to church
You can't make me
You can't force me to go
You can't take me

What is God?
Who is God?
This may sound strange to you
But it's not odd

Church participation is diminishing
It's fading away
I know what's going on
The devil is leading us astray

God is watching
God knows how we treat each other
God is listening
God knows how we greet each other

Sometime God shakes us up
God gives us a little scare
To make us see
To make us aware

Don't do that
That's not right
Open your eyes
Follow my light

I'm not ignoring the advice
That you whisper in my ear
I hear you God
I hear you loud and clear

## I Know God

Resist the devil
The one below
God
Is whom you need to know

God loves me
God is always there
God will not forsake me
God was there
When I'm down and out
The Lord's guidance
Removed my doubt

God is my direction
I follow his lead
The Lord provides me with the Holy
Spirit
God continues to feed

I'm down on my knees
Praying to thee
I'm calling
This prayer is from me

Resist the devil
The one below
God
Is whom you need to know

## The Mark that You Left

I'm not the same person anymore
I'm better
The mark that you left
Will be with me forever

I was down
I was weak
I called out to you
It was help that I seek

You came to me
In my dark hour
I feel your strength
I feel your power

Thank you God
For saving me
The mark that you left
Has set me free

I'm not the same person anymore
I'm better
The mark that you left
Will be with me forever

## Thinking about Church

Now I realize
Now I know
Church
The place where I can always go

When I think about church
I think about grace
When I think about church
A smile appears on my face

Dealing with all kinds of stuff
During the week
Dealing with this stuff
Makes me weak

When I think about church
I think of peace
The Monday through Saturday
madness stops
Or cease

When I think about church
That's the place to be
When I think about church
I'm filled with so much glee

Church
I love going there
I enjoy hearing the word of God
In church- I feel the Holy Spirit
everywhere

Now I realize
Now I know
Church
The place where I can always go

# I'm Praying For My Life Back

I'm praying for my life back
The life I had before
I'm craving this
More and more

## I'm Praying For My Life Back

I'm praying for my life back
The life I had before
I'm craving this
More and more

Our father
The one up high
Let me know
Before I die

I don't understand
I need you guide
I'm walking around with a wet face
Tears I don't hide

So much hate in my heart
I have a lot
I'm so angry
I'm red hot

So much pain in my heart
I feel too much
I feel every abusive touch
It hurts so much

Our father
I'm asking why
Why did she die?
All they do is lie

I don't even try
To believe anymore
I'm alone again
Like once before

I don't trust you anymore
I only trust me
My door is locked
And I only have one key

No one may enter
Chances they have blown
A new me is here
This is now known

I've shown you signs
I was getting you prepared
I'm not afraid anymore
I'm not scared

Our father
Many lives taken
I'm down on my knees
Because you I was forsaken

Our father
I'm struggling
I don't make a lot of money
I'm struggling

When I do make some money
It goes away
So many bills and debt
I have to pay

Our father
Why are they attacking me?
He and she is attacking me
Everyone is attacking me

My heart is good
That's what they see
I leave myself open
They always mistreat me

Our father
You know me well
I yell at you
Every time I fail

Our father
I have no heart beat
Love was in front
Now it's in the back seat

Our father
There's something wrong with me
The world we live in now
Have definitely changed me

I was on top of my game
Without a care
Then something happened
That took away all my care

I lost my soul
I don't know where to go
I'm walking around in a circle
I'm moving very slow

Our father
I hear the countdown
Every night I wake up with a cold sweat
And a frightful frown

There's an illness in my family
It's getting bad
I'm trying to hold myself together
I feel so sad

No weapon against me shall prosper
God told me this
God also said
You will have limited bliss

It's like that now
It was like that in the beginning
People mistreat me
Always winning

It's not over yet
It's not over at all
Soon
Those against me will fall

Goliath fell
David took him out
I know in the end
I'll win the final bout

You don't know about my hurt
I feel this deep
I feel it when I'm awake
And when I sleep

My heart is filled with pain
All I see is rain
Because my eyes is filled with tears
Right now I have a lot of fears
I don't hear any more cheers

Once galore
Now misery
Once a poet
Now that's history

So much hurt
Everyday I feel it
So much hurt
It's hard to conceal it

So much hurt
Do you hear what I say?
Pain
Harass me everyday

I'm praying for my life back
The life I had before
I'm craving this
More and more

## I Told God I'll Be Back

I've told you before
I'm off track
I told God
I'll be back

I told God I'll be back
I'm not myself right now
Opposite
I'm somebody else right now

I told God I'll be back
Because I want to go to heaven
God
Please show me the way to heaven

Righteousness
What does that mean?
I'm doing wrong
I'm being mean

Evil
I'm not civil
Devilish
I'm so sinful

I told God I'll be back
Strife has changed me
Misery
Won't let me be

Save me
Set me free
Lord
I need to be with thee

I told God I'll be back
I'm searching for
That door
Explore
Until I find
Some peace
Inside my mind

I've told you before
I'm off track
I told God
I'll be back

## Run With Patience

You're not done
You've just begun
Use patience
When you run

The Lord said, run with patience
The road ahead is tough
You will encounter a lot of bumps
The surface is rough

The Lord said, run with patience
Because the road is long
Your journey is lengthy
You have to be strong

The wrong direction
You will be tempted to go
Run with patience
Take it slow

The Lord said, run with patience
This is your journey
You have to pray
And believe in me

I am your path
I am your light
I will show you how to do right

You're not done
You've just begun
Use patience
When you run

## Reading The Bible

Teach me Lord
I don't want to be idle
I'm reading the bible

Jesus is the author and finisher of our faith
Who for the joy that was set before him endured the cross despising the shame
And is set down at the right hand of the throne of God
Jesus, I will always praise your name

For all who have sinned
Come short of the glory of God
Know ye no that the righteous
Shall inherit the kingdom of God
The wicked shall be turned into hell
And all nations that forget God
For they, being ignorant of God's righteousness
And going about to establish their own righteousness
Have not submitted themselves unto righteousness of God

By the word of God
I'm reborn
Once a lost soul
Once tormented and scorn

Being born again by the word of God
Which liveth and abideth forever
Love one another with a pure heart
Make this love last forever

The word of the Lord is the word
By which the gospel is preached
unto you
Some know this
Others don't have a clue

Love one another
With a heart that's pure
Lord give me strength
So I can endure

Abstain from fleshly lusts
Which wars against the soul
Lord heal me
Because I have a hurt soul

Teach me Lord
I don't want to be idle
I'm reading the bible

## I'm Incomplete

I need you
I'm kneeling at your feet
I'm broken
I'm incomplete

I only pick up the bible on Sunday
I only read the bible on Sunday
I only think about church on
Sunday

The suffering of this present time
Are not worthy to be compared with
the glory which shall be revealed in
us
Heaven is my direction
God loves all of us

When you live by the spirit of God
You become a child of God
You will become a messenger of God
You will be in heaven with God

If I may touch but his clothes
I shall be whole
Let me touch you Jesus
Make me whole

Jesus, said thy faith hath made me whole
Go in peace
I feel different now
I feel so much peace

My faith made me whole
My faith made me complete
You can see the change in me
Whenever we meet

The Lord said, go in peace
Peace be with you
Lord grant me serenity
I need this from you

I need you
I'm kneeling at your feet
I'm broken
I'm incomplete

## Speak Up And Talk

I give to thee in the name of Jesus
Jesus said, rise and walk
Jesus said, don't be afraid
Speak up and talk

"I am your voice"
"Tell them what I said"
His words come to me often
Especially when I'm asleep in bed

Blessed is the man that endured temptation
For when he is tried, he shall receive the crown of life
The Lord promise this to him
He will have a life without strife

For let not man think that he shall receive anything of the Lord
Let no man say when he is tempted,
I am tempted of God; for God cannot be tempted with evil
Neither tempted by any man
Lord, please show me how to be a Christian man

But every man is tempted
When he is drawn away of his own
entice and lust
Lord your guidance I need
This is a must

Then when lust hath conceived it
bringeth for sin
And sin when it is finished bringeth
forth death
Lord, I'm a sinner
My conclusion is death

I need you
To take me to the next level
Right now I'm stuck with the devil

I give to thee in the name of Jesus
Jesus said, rise and walk
Jesus said, don't be afraid
Speak up and talk

## The Devil Goes To Church

For all of those who are clueless
This will help you know
Church
The devil go

The devil goes to church
The devil is sitting next to me
The devil is he or she

The devil goes to church
The devil is talking in my ear
Telling me
That I don't need to be here

The devil goes to church
The devil told me to get up and walk
out
The devil is trying to fill me with
doubt

Praising God on Sunday
Monday through Saturday raising
hell
Pretending to be a Christian
Everyone does this very well

We are not perfect saints
The Lord knows this
Church prepares us for everlasting
love, peace, and bliss

It's hard being a Christian
In this time and day
Because the devil is leading the way
And we follow
Fooled by tricks
The devil wants us down below

For all of those who are clueless
This will help you know
Church
The devil go

## **Spiritual High**

I'm trying to stop my tears
I don't want to cry
I'm empty inside
I need a spiritual high

I'm walking around
Mind filled with doubt
I'm very bitter
I want to shout
So you can hear my anger
I feel like a worm on a fishing hook
And life is the dangler

I need some money
I'm scheming and plotting
I'm recalling the way people treat me
They're low down, dirty and rotten

I'm spotting
Trying to find my place
So many mistakes
I need to erase

Don't look at my face
Don't look at me
My vulnerability
I don't want you to see

I'm weak
Right now I'm not strong
I'm surrounded by temptation
I'm doing something wrong

The days are long
The nights are cold
I'm falling apart
Loneliness is bold

I can't sleep
So many nightmares
Eyes always watching
Constant stares

I'm paranoid
I'm always watching my back and front
Will you please be quiet?
Why do you taunt?

In front of me, there's a church
Should I go in?
There's a tug of war going on
The right way and sin

I'm looking inside the church's window
There's a bible on a stand
This is a sign
God is reaching out his hand

I'm trying to stop my tears
I don't want to cry
I'm empty inside
I need a spiritual high

## **Putting My Life Back Together**

Stay with me God
I will do better
You're the reason I'm still here
I need some time to put my life back together

Sinful ways
That's a part of me
I'm not perfect
I'm not holy

People judge me
Because I don't act like a saint
They want a perfect picture
This is hard to paint

The bad stuff that I do
The things I'm not suppose to do
I haven't learned my lesson yet
I continue to do
It's hard to change
Doing what's right
Feels strange

Going to church on Sundays
Lord please forgive me
Give me another chance
The devil won't flee
He's always there
His temptation is strong
He's everywhere
He won't leave
Have faith in God
I must believe

Give me strength God
I'm so weak
Help me
It's you that I seek

I have many flaws
I'm doing a lot of bad
I don't like the way I am
Deep down inside I'm sad

The stuff that I've done and do
Is wrong
It's on me to change
This battle I'm fighting is long
It will always last
I have a lot of problems now
I can't run away from my past

Who am I?
I simply don't know
I've lost my direction
I don't know where to go

Talk is cheap
I'm not changing my mind
I'm in too deep
It's hard to rewind
I'm not going back
The person I use to be is gone
He's not coming back

I'm thrown off track
I have no control
I seek redemption
Because I lost my soul

I have to clean myself
To get rid of the dirt in my life
This means the more wrong I do
The more strife

Stay with me God
I will do better
You're the reason I'm still here
I need some time to put my life back together

## **Heaven**

Heaven
I want to see this place
I want to see Jesus
I want to see God's face

Heaven
I can't wait to get there
I'm ready to receive God's love and care

Heaven
The place for me
Heaven
The place where I'm truly free

Heaven
I'm almost there
Where worry doesn't exist
Not even one care

Heaven
I'm almost here
I'm not afraid to die anymore
I have no fear

Heaven
I'm ready for God's embrace
I'm ready to rest now
Because it's been a long race

Heaven
There is no pain
A place where I can relax
Because I'm tired of the pain

Heaven
Please let me in
God forgive me
Forgive me when I sin
Heaven
Will I go?
Am I going to make it?
God will let me know

Heaven
I've passed the test
It's my time to go
It's my time to rest

Heaven
I want to see this place
I want to see Jesus
I want to see God's face

## Is there a Place for Me In Heaven?

Is there a place for me in heaven?
I really need to know
Is heaven my destination?
Will I go?

Is there a place for me in heaven?
This question constantly runs
through my mind
You know that my heart has been
hateful lately
But I'm good and kind

God is there a place for me in
heaven?
Is there a spot for me?
I don't want to dwell in hell
It's too hot for me

I'm not perfect God
I sin
Please forgive me God
Please let me in

Listen to me God
Please don't ignore
Is there a place for me in heaven?
Will I reach heaven's door?

Is there a place for me in heaven?
I really need to know
Is heaven my destination?
Will I go?

## My Story to Date...

Jason O'Neal Williams was born in Houston, Texas on July 21, 1978. He lived there for 8 years. He and his family later moved to Homer, Louisiana. He attended Homer High school and Grambling State University. Both schools are in Louisiana. He graduated from Homer High School in 1996 and Grambling State University on May 19, 2002 with a Bachelors of Science degree in marketing. At the tender age of 23, he began writing poetry. He started writing poetry at a dark point in his life. He started writing poetry in 2001. He started writing poetry his last year in college. Before a recurring dream, he had no interest in poetry and didn't take any poetry classes. He was having the same dream night after night for three days straight. When he awoke from the first dream, he decided to write about it because it was so intense.

When he wrote about the dream, it came out in a rhyme. He didn't pay any attention to the dream or poem because he thought it was a fluke or mistake. The next night, same dream another and different rhyme. The next night, same dream another and different rhyme. He kept having the same dream with different points of views about it. His response to those dreams was poetry. That dream changed and saved his life. Before the dream he was frustrated, depressed, and stressed out. He was ready to give up on himself and life. He was very suicidal. After that experience, he knew something special was happening to him. This was something that he could avoid or ignore.

At first he was afraid of this talent. He didn't understand what was happening to him. Because waking one day with a talent that you never had before can scare anyone. With a little more time and his faith in God, he finally understood and accepted it.

From that moment on, he was never the same. He became another person, "The Prince of Poetry". He has the ability to change the world and make a difference. And he fully accepts the responsibility that he has. God gave him this gift to help him deal with life. God gave him this gift to help others as well. God gave him this gift at the time he needed it. Mr. Williams has been writing poetry for 5 years now.

On March 2002, he attended and competed at the International Poetry convention in Orlando, Florida. The convention was held at the world famous Disney Coronado Springs Resort, located in Walt Disney World. The convention included workshops, seminars, readings, rap sessions, poetry contests and poetry critiques. It was a great experience for him.

He learned a lot about his craft. It was basically three days of non-stop poetry and entertainment. He had the chance to meet different poets from all over the world. He didn't win the poetry competition but it didn't discourage him. It just boosted his determination and drive to be the best poet he could be. That day he promised himself that he was not going to let anything or anyone stand in his way from becoming a poet and a published author.

Also in 2002, he was nominated for International Poet of the year and received the 2002 International Poet of Merit award. He also received the 2002 Editor's choice award for his poem "I Want To Succeed". He also has 3 poems published in other poetry anthologies, Silent Solitude (2002), New Millennium Poets (2002) and 2004 International Who's Who In Poetry (2004). He was the only American featured poet for that year.

In 2003 at the age of 24, he made his debut as an author with his first book of poetry called "My Story, Through My Eyes". This book is based on his life. It's about his experiences, thoughts and feelings. It was published by Publish America. Mr. Williams has done a lot in such a short time. He has another book of poetry called, "E.3" (Experiencing Death, Emotional Disturbance, Everlasting Love) May 2004.

This book was also published by Publish America. This book is the sequel to "My Story, Through My Eyes." It is the continuation of the story. It's about life, his life, and the life of others. This book is more personal. It shows his maturity and vulnerability as a person, poet and writer. This book is filled with unbelievable emotion.

Jason released 2 books in 2005, The Life That I Live and I Must Confess, The Lost Pages. The Life That I Live is a collection of writing. It consists of poetry, fiction and nonfiction. It is also a play. All of these parts come together to tell one story. This book is about a fictional African American character Jamal Johnson. Jamal is a poet, professional writer, teacher and author. This story is about Jamal's ups and downs.

I Must Confess, The Lost Pages is a book of poetry. This book contains missing poetry from Jason's first 2 books of poetry, My Story, Through My Eyes and E.3 (Experiencing Death, Emotional Disturbance, Everlasting Love). This book also contains new poetry.

Jason's 5th book, 2 Sides To A Story, is now available. This book of poetry was written by Shena Henderson and Jason O'Neal Williams. This story is about Shena's and Jason's life. This book is about their experiences (past and present). This book is about their variety of thoughts and feelings.

Prince Jason, "Welcome to My Kingdom" is Jason's 6th book. This book of poetry is the continuation of his life story. 7 is Mr. Williams 7th book. He continues to tell write and talk about the life that he lives. J.B.3 is Jason's 8th published book. This is a children's book about 3 African American brothers who are superheroes. Jason's 9th book is a J.B.3 coloring book.

Mr. Williams is a talented person, poet, and writer. He is a young man with a special gift. He has a gift that others can benefit from. He has the ability to change, inspire, encourage, or influence. He has the potential of becoming great someday. This is only the beginning for him. There's a lot more to come in the future.

# Author's Accomplishments

## Jason O'Neal Williams

## "Prince Jason"

## The Prince of Poetry

- 2002 International Poet Of The Year nominee
- 2002 International Poet Of Merit Award
- January 2002 Editor's Choice Award
- 2002 Inductee of The International Society of Poets
- First appearance in Ebony magazine (November 2003 issue) on page 201.
- 2003 Member of the Writers' League of Texas (Austin, Texas)
- 2004 Pinkie Carolyn Wilkerson award for poetry- presented by Grambling State University
- 2004 International Who's Who In Poetry-The only American featured poet for that year

- 2006 Pinkie Carolyn Wilkerson award for poetry- presented by Grambling State University
- 2006 Poetry writer for Black College Today Magazine
- 2008 Poetry Editor for Starving Writers Publishing
- 2008 appearance in the movie Harold and Kumar 2

Made in the USA